Spoken:
The Art of Words

By: Victor

These words are dedicated to Life for showing me Love, Laughter, and some heartache. Through failure and success, I was allowed to learn and grow, and I will continue to do so.

Foreword

Being more pensive than verbally expressive, it's no wonder that we are all being privy to his most inner thoughts in written form entitled "Spoken". Preferring, rather than to ask questions, to bear witness to human interaction by donning earbuds releasing no sound in the midst of everyday life order to capture mental pictures of human emotion in its rawest form. This is much more than merely the thoughts of the poet. This is a reflection of all of our thoughts projected back to us through his lens. So like a train ride thru the city of Chicago from which he hails, taking in the richness of soaring skyscrapers, jazz and blues clubs, he invites you to sit back and ride through his mental flows. Some stops will be familiar. Others, brand new. But all resounding with the beat of a heart that will, inevitably, resonate with each and every one of us.

- L. M. Leach

Time

It's said that time
Heals all wounds
And I ask you
Who clocks time
Festering has been this wound of mine
Daily injections of antibiotics
Called hope
Antidepressants take shape
In forms of wonder
Side effects are countless
Forever scrolling across the bottom
Of my life's screen
Warning
May cause further heartbreak
Warning
May cause anger
Warning
May cause bitterness
Warning
May cause a tight chest
Due to stress
Warning *Warning* *Warning*

My chest is not tight due to stress
There's a surgical wound
That can't be soothed
See that scar there
Is where my heart was removed
Or should I say ripped out
Every stitch
Has a memory attached to it
Promises have become empty
Blueprints and licenses
Are now demolition projects and permits
Future building is only for constructing walls
Around this barren space
That once held my whole world
Because that's all I have left
And if I can somehow
Keep this area open
I can reflect on the remnants
Of the love that condemned me
For not being good enough
My life stands still
While everyone is moving by
At a rapid climb
Again, I ask you, who clocks time?

Social Media

No longer do we stop and stare
We tweet
No longer can we tell the kids
Of the places we'd first meet
It's like, I was watching my favorite
TV show
And she poked me
Then I poked her back
Then we started having the battle
Of the "poke" war attack
To see who would get the last one
That's what we have to tell the kids
We called having fun
Then after a week or so
I'd finally say hi my name is Victor
Like you didn't already know
And I ask you for your name
Like I just can't read the screen
Simple pleasantries
Destroyed by technology
The search goes away...
It's from going out to the nights end
To "Oh look we have mutual friends"

So lets pretend that's what we connect on
And if we start a relationship
To make it less awkward
Let's say that we met through a friend
And then let's go out
Because you have to be safe
We know the same person
And they wouldn't harm a fly
Except that one time when he said
That all must die
But nevertheless, let's go anyway
Lets go to a restaurant and sit
And stare at each other
And say nothing
I'm scratching my head
And wondering why there
Is no sound coming out of you
You just wrote me a book in
Message form the other day
Now it's nothing for you to say
So we result in going to Facebook
To look at other people's statuses
And talk about them
I'm looking at your page to see
Why you don't look the same
(Damn you Instagram)

What light were you in
Because we need to match it.
This is tragic
Your personality does not
Fit your status
Wait did you just post
You were having a great time?
With who??
It says it here 5secs ago
I wish I could delete you with one click in person
Like I can on here because this...
Wait did you just change your relationship status
And tag me in it?
It says it here 5 secs ago
No, we aren't doing this
I got to leave
Waiter bring the check please...

This, is where we are these days
We lost all personal attributes
We create fantasies with
The tip of our fingers
What happened to the times
When people use to linger
Around other people
Just to see if they can
Hear a funny joke

Now.... all we do is post
Or tweet
Reality check
You really don't have 500 friends
Two at best
You are not a real photographer
Your pictures are blurry
And no, Bill Gates will not give you a million dollars
If you share his picture...

Our head's constantly facing downward
With interference between
This person and the next
We walk around lifeless
Then wonder why kids
Don't place much value in theirs
And when you talk to them
All you get is blank stares
And murmurs from their lips
Truth is......
We are the zombie apocalypse

Every Year

Disgusted

Scared

Numb

Tired of tears

Body's slain

Hash tagged name

Because of your fears

Families

Pained

Souls

Drained

Every

Single

Year

My Problem with the 'Conscious' Community

So I thought the whole purpose
Of waking up
Was to be free
Not to be bound
By other traditions
That move with
Religious similarities

Your hallelujahs
Have become Ases
Your 'Assalamualaikums'
Now, hoteps
Your crosses
Your star and crescents
Are now ankhs

So fast to fall in another line
Thinking that's where you should be
Quickly forgetting the reason
You woke up was to be free
Not to be tied up
By another belief

Now we can talk about Mohammed
Or we could switch to Jesus

Krishna, Mithras, Oedipus,
Same story right?
Even all the way back to Heru
But that doesn't mean they're for us to follow
Or could it be too hard to swallow
That if one of them existed the others did too
I know knowledge has it's need
Say what you gotta say
Then walk away
Just drop that seed
Understand that everyone doesn't
Learn at the same speed
No need to shit
On another person's belief

I get it you're conscious or woke
But get out of the way
You just came into this knowledge yesterday
Stop the self gratification
You know, the mental masturbation
Only the application of information
Can be your proof

All things are subject to interpretation
Whichever interpretation prevails at a given time

Is a function of power, not truth
The information you come into
Could be just for you

Whoever subscribes the diameter of your learning,
Controls the circumference of your thinking.

So question everything
The beginning of knowledge
Is when you start unlearning
What's been programmed into you

You don't blame the computer
For the virus uploaded into it
Just like you can't blame the magician
When you know it's all tricks

Let's treat each other with
Compassion, love and understanding
Because when you get down to it
That's the nature of it
Don't let your knowledge get in the way

Ase

Fathers

For the dad that teaches courage
For the father that teaches discipline
For the dad that says I love you
For the father that tucks you in

For the dad that reads you a bedtime story
For the father who gives God all the glory
For the dad who showed you hard-work
For the father that protected you from the jerks

For the dad who eased the hurt and pain
For the father that taught you the game
For the dad who told you no
For the father that helped you grow

For the father that was and is driven crazy
From dealing with drama
From the mother of the baby

For the dad who tried to make it right
The unseen fight night after night
For the father who couldn't see
An end in sight
For the father who gave up
And wished he never did

For the dad that left
Because it was best for the kid

For the dad who's in jail with a case
Doing everything he can
So his son won't take his place

For the dad who calls everyday
With nothing really to say
For the father who admitted his mistake
And is trying to heal the wound of heartbreak

For the dad that's on the right track
For the father not letting anything
hold him back
For the ones that need to make a u-turn
And go the other way
There's no day like today
To get it right
And make it stay

For the father for the dad
For you who are happy
For those who are sad

For those who need their relationship to bloom
For that man who realizes they're
A father everyday
Not just a Sunday in June

Back in the Day

Back in the day when I was young
I'm not a kid anymore
But some days I sit and wish
I was a kid again
And I remember way back when
I remember way back
When the only ninjas were turtles
And they had Shredder to attack
I remember way back when
I thought I had all the power
By yelling "Thunder, Thunder, Thundercats!!!"
I remember way back when
Life was so sweet
And the only question I needed an answer for
Was can you tell me how to get
How to get to Sesame Street
I remember way back when
Reading Rainbow came on
I turned it up like it was my favorite song
I remember way back when
Rap made you feel good
Just like an R&B song could
When your only line for that chick to mack
Was from that album cover with the lyrics on the back
"When I'm alone in my room sometimes I stare at the wall

And in the back of my mind I hear my conscience call"
LL needed love
And at that moment
For some reason I needed it too
I remember way back when
It was fun to give mud pies
To your best friend
When fireworks were fun to ignite
4th of July had the hood looking so bright
Don't forget about the streetlight
Y'all remember that was curfew
And you better be on the porch
And say bye to your friends before momma do
I remember back in the day when
There was no Xbox nor Play station
If you could see the light of day
Outside was the only way to play
Imagination, Simon says
Red light Green light, Hide and Seek
Freeze tag
Screaming 'not it'
Or Everybody put your foot in
Engine Engine #9 going down the County line
And if that train goes off the track do you want
Your money back
Universal games that were free
Had everyone in the hood

Happy as can be
Maybe you had your own
And maybe that was the last time you had fun
Because you got too grown
Just about the time you got that pager
Or that Zack Morris Phone
Whatever it was I think we got it too fast
Because the kids now
Are on a fast track to crash
There's no more outside playing
There's no more Mother May I sayings
Their mind is being shaped
Instead of roaming free
Forget A.D.H.D
Kids are suffering from
L.O.C
Lack of Creative disease
Parents listen please
Establish an environment for them
So that creation marries mystery
And as they get older
They will then
Have their own
"I remember way back when"

Everybody say
I remember way back when
And everybody say
Back in the day
Back in the day

Dad

You never really get over it
You just learn to live with it
Holding on being strong
Cuz the guy who helped
Give me life is gone

The years of absentee
Seem so small now
The past two years
The relationship grew
Strong somehow

I don't know about you
But when a piece of you
Is going through
You're praying until they're healed
All the pride drops
Attitude falls off your shoulder
You realize that you love them still
Even for all the BS
You said you'd never get over.

I grew older and wisdom I grasped
As my maturity level boosts,
I realized the past was the past
At one time I wanted to hold up a fist
Now it's a handshake that I ask
Or a hug or just for you to call out my name
Or ring my phone even if I'm not home
So I can see the missed call or
Hear the message you left.
Your voice, on repeat
Your laughter, one last time
The silly jokes and funny looks that
Only we understand
Are forever embedded in my mind
I sit outside and look up at the night's sky
Wondering what star you passed by
On your way to the gates where Peter stands
He extended his hand and you two shook
With every quiet step you took
You walk into Heaven
Because your name is in the book.

Have You Seen Her

Oh I see her face everywhere I go
In streets even at the picture show
Have you seen her
Tell me have you seen...

Of course you haven't
Cause you don't look
From right up under our noses
Ours girls get took

What's happening around the world
That makes our girls go missing
They're either stolen
Or classified as runaways
We are failing our mission

Is no one paying attention?
A runaway is still a stolen girl
Mentally she lost a battle
There's no more innocence in her world

Have you seen her
Tell me have you seen her
I hear her voice as the cool winds blow
Oh the sweet music on the radio
Have you seen her

Or...
Maybe the music is bitter
She gets her image off twitter
Instagram fame
Don't know her real name
Down for the team or a quitter

ABC rappers
Aka trappers
We never gave them permission
To give our girls fictitious definitions
Of what they are suppose to be

No real security
Distracted by Reality TV
Tablets and phones
That's why when we look up
Another one is gone

Parenting is hard
And does not come with a manual
Understand if you're lacking in some area
They will too
So they really won't listen to what you say
They'll just follow what you do

Have you seen her
Tell me have you seen her

It seems like we don't care
The black market thrives off us
Not being there
Sex trafficking
Organ harvesting
Drug running
Our little girls participating
In things we can't even imagine

Growing up we were told
That a child should be seen
And not heard
Well that's absurd
Because we're so distracted now
We're not looking
And we definitely don't listen
Until they come up missin

There's no more milk carton
Only Amber alerts
And sometimes we get the Ebony
But knowing what you know now
That shouldn't surprise you
Walking around
Different shades of gold
They want to get their hands on you

Like a pimp
They'll start
With the heart
Then sell the rest of her body parts

KDM

I remember when she first told me
A 2004 Florida's summer
The night was nice
Moon was full
I was semi homeless
Nonetheless this conversation
Sticks with me best
In emotional distress
By the time the conversation ended

She reached out to me
I dropped the ball
It was heavy
Busy dealing with my life changes
And I wasn't ready

You're what?!?!?
Whoa!!!!
When did this happen?!!??
You weren't raised this way?!!?!
What price does this family have to pay?!?!

I ruined this relationship drastically
It was all about my loss

Well I'll never be...
I'll never have the chance to...

I didn't understand what
She had to go thru
The confusion, stares and dirty looks
Being told how it was all a phase
Just give her this "good" book
Maybe she'd get the bigger picture
If you point to this scripture

In that moment
I didn't observe her vulnerability
I didn't see how her relationship with me
Would affect her other realities
I was probably viewed as her biggest resister

And I couldn't visualize then
That she just wanted to be my friend
She still wanted to be
Most importantly
My Sister

Granny

It's happened before
But this one hurts more
It's like
I'm reshuffling the deck
In hopes for better cards or
Trying to deal away the pain
But it's seems that I'm stuck
With the same....
Hand
The dealer's playing spades
But I'm all heart
Wearing emotions on my sleeve
Is where it all starts
Memories are told by the tears
That appear on my face
Rolling down every inch of my skin
There's a drop of memories within
From the food to the games
The conversations
And the silly names
The laughter and jokes
The times you brought me
Change to count from the riverboats

The cobblers,
The cherry and the peach
The times you said wretch but
We knew you meant reach
The bingo, keno or Trip-o-ly
Didn't need money
Just chips and the can of pennies
Granny, you will be missed
With all the thrown fits
The hug, the kiss
All the food you graciously
Gave to neighbors
On the other side of the fence
The holiday dinner runs
From the youngest one
Getting beer & pop for all the guests
Oh.... the memories
And these are just clips
Like a trailer to a movie....

Going up and down the stairs
Now....
You'll no longer be there
But I'll still do it when I go home
I'll still call your phone
I'll still lie in your bed
Waiting for you to scratch my head

Just like I did before I got all grown
Only this time I know it won't come
You always said nothing lasts forever.
So I'm glad the pain
Didn't take the pleasure
Of making you suffer long...
We'll grow stronger as the days go by
No matter how many tears we cry
No matter how many years we try
December 25th will forever
Have a different meaning, you see
The best present you've given
No matter how I was livin'
Was your love to me!

Edith R. Rand

August 28, 1923 - December 25, 2013

This Bitch is My Mother and Yours Too

She has her favorites
I'm not one of them
I take it personal
I plead for her to love me
Like she does her other children
But it falls on deaf ears
Which brings me to tears
For I fear how this will effect my up bringing
And how I'd raise my kids
And how I also interact with my other siblings
But I just want to love her
Like any child should love their parent
And I want her to love me
I thought that's how family should be
But she keeps me at a distance
For instance
A long time ago,
I was getting bullied
By my brothers and sisters
Every single day
I was condemned
For my retaliation
Like I always got caught throwing the punch
So she'd think I'm was the one starting it

But I'm like 'Mom it was in defense,
I'm just playing my part in it'
She wasn't hearing me
Turned a blind eye to shit
Referred to me as her wild child
Said I was always aggressive
Embarrassed me in front of her friends
Like I was a terror
She'd say hey look
Here goes my little super predator

Punishment came
I'm talking long timeouts too
Mandatory minimum
Days months years it's true
Sibling rivalries
Always got the best of me
Then one day I got older
Seemed like I had my chest to beat
To prove to her
"I'm not what you said I'd be"
But she already put the fear
In the other members of my family
So no matter what I said
It sounded like "woe is me"
But I'm trying to tell about

How momma held them comfortably
But she held me..... back
Arrested my development
Threw my life off track
About how she gave them
Keys to the kingdom
But gave my kingdom crack
I wanted gold too
It was my inherent right
But she kept us at each other
Secretly enticing fights

This bitch is my mother
But she's yours too
I'm not her favorite
I'm your brother but we're not equal
Momma always changed her clothes
But she never took a bath
Splashing perfume on stink
End up smelling worst than dead ass
Now I can call her out every time she does this
But she pays me no mind
Her ears only hear from her favorites
And those who have money
She always tries to silence me
But she can no longer quiet my voice

So I end this poem abruptly
By asking you to
Go talk to momma for me
Ask her to love all her children equally
Because pretty soon
She loses her choice

Hearts

Hearts are wild creatures
That's why our ribs are cages
Locked up for ages
Ready to bust out
And go on to its natural way
To meet its natural mate

She Said Goodbye to Him

She said goodbye to him
Even though she said she loved him
She said goodbye to him
Even though she knew
The pain they'd both go through
She said goodbye
Maybe with tear filled eyes
I don't know but
She said goodbye to him
She refrained from the kiss
That sent them to heart filled
Lands and dream spaces
She said goodbye to him
With dinner, wine and conversations
The things they both longed for
Are not happening anymore
She said goodbye to him
Even though the essence
Is still lingering
The passion is still tingling
Even though she knew
That she made him come alive
She said goodbye
Now his heart slowly dies

Beginning his search
For soft burial ground
For a love like this
Will never again be found
He sends one last note
Before being lowered down
Asking for her to return her prize
To place his heart in the box
Next to the tears he's cried
She said goodbye to him

Mothers

This poem is for the mothers
The mother who got out of the bed
At the drop of a dime
Every time she heard a whimper or whine

This poem is for the mother who lost her hourglass shape
And coke bottle frame just to give us life
And to give us a name

This poem is for the mother who stood her ground
And did not back down at anytime
When someone said bad things about her child

This poem is for the mother who helped with the homework
Even though she knew nothing about algebra or science
This poem is for the mother who didn't become her kid's friend
And disciplined them for defiance

This poem is for the mother who went to
Every parent teacher conference
Who stood by and still loved her child
In spite of all the nonsense

This poem, this poem is for the mothers who
Took a father's place and
Held back the hate to
Try and raise the son that had the daddy's face and
Had the daddy's smile and
She held back her tongue when he
Came over for a while "just to kick it"

This poem is for the mother who held down two jobs
Just for her baby to have a childhood and not feel robbed

This poem is for the mother who never complained and
Tried to stay sane when her unwed daughter came
Home... with... an... enlarged stomach

This poem is for the mother who lost her child
Whether to drugs, alcohol, suicide or murder
Maybe it was jail or disease
This poem is for the mother who had and
Who wants this pain eased

This poem is for the mother
Who is in her prayer closet
Every chance she gets, down her knees

When her baby's fighting overseas
And every time a car pulls up she's hoping it's them

This poem is for the mother who
Stuck it out with the father just for the child
Who had every reason to leave when dad was acting wild

This poem is for the mothers
Who took care of us like no others

This poem is for the mothers who found strength in God
And is obedient even though it feels kinda odd
And gives her tithe and offerings
And never has a need, when she plants that seed

This poem is for the mother who
Despite all our shortcomings
Encouraged us faithfully
To be all that we can be

This poem is for you
I thank you
The men thank you
We love you

Summer Love

Cool wind
In a summer's breeze
She's got the type of love
That would bring
Any man to his knees

I Remember Her

I remember her
I was married so
I couldn't extend to her
Previous pleasures
Familiar to her
One simple hello and
There we'd go
Clothes on the floor
Cops got neighbors knocking on our door

Yeah I remember her
Her intentions
She hid it from her face
But never her taste
She'd call
I'd pick a place
Less than 10
Hopped in the car and meetin
Car rides led to slow glides
And my hands up and down her thighs
No alleys
Just hills and valleys
Where I directed the flow of the rivers

I remember her
Her focus
100% on me
Locked into each other's needs
From conversations
And touching ones mind
To touching ones soul
With just a caress
With one kiss
We'd touch one another's hearts
Until one had to depart
And we'd do this all the time
And in the moment it was so divine
I remember her
Constantly
In my head
Wishing she'd be in my bed
Lying around just talking
About any and everything
All the joy she brings
To my imagination
When I couldn't see her
So I end up just walking
Around the city
Hoping we bump into each other
So I could pick a place

Then off we'd go
To experience the unknown
Until the moon sent us home

I remember her
I had this feeling that
Together we'd rule the world
Emotions on high
Consistent flow
Time moving fast
Only the love making was slow
Intense moans
In merging moments
The fragrance we created
Kept us going
Yes I remember her

I remember her
Sparks flying when we embraced
A dictionary and AirBnB
Just in case
I remember her like the 4th of July
And even tho she doesn't
Celebrate Holidays
I remember the fireworks
When I looked into her eyes
I remember her

Time Goes By

Time goes by slower
No communication
Makes it longer
I neither hear your voice
Nor can I see you
Makes days tough to get through

Where are you
Are you staring at the same
Stars as I
I hope you're having fun
I hope I still
Reside
In your heart

If This Is Goodbye

If this is goodbye
Let me stay with you
Until the sunrise

If this is goodbye
Let me wipe one last tear
From your eyes
If this is goodbye

If this is goodbye
Take my hand
And squeeze it tightly
Remind me of the way
I held you nightly
If this is goodbye

If this is goodbye
Look at me with the love
I've come to know
Lie to me
Tell me you won't let go
Gaze into my eyes
Help me keep away
The lonely cries
If this is goodbye

If this is goodbye
Travel with me
Back to a time
Where our souls were intertwined
And your legs wrapped around
The divinity of love

If this is goodbye
Talk to me sweetly
Take away this bitter taste
Of pain and broken dreams
Put our songs on repeat
Dance with me
Until the soles of my feet
Match my bleeding heart
If this is goodbye

If this is goodbye
Don't say it
Fade into the night's sky
My heart still needs you
My spirit still longs for you
My eyes still tear
At the thought of you being

So if this is goodbye
Don't say it
Just fade into the....
Just fade into...
Just fade...
Just.....

If Only

Whopper or Big Mac
Whatever her favorite snack
If only she'd remember
The loving things daddy said
She wouldn't be caught dead
Opening her legs for meat and bread
Not even a coke and a smile
Would be a gateway
For her body to be defiled

The Fire We Make

It's about to get hot in here
For you
I'm already disrobed
And I've come to unclothe
You...
Let my words assume the position
Of my hands
And twist your body in a subtle trance
Side to side back and forth
Back and forth and side to side
Feel the temperature rise
As I pull you closer to me
Stroking you gently
Admiring your assets...
You call flaws
Complementing the beauty...
You call scars
Caressing your body with sweet phrases
Connecting all your dots
Starting and finishing all your mazes
Getting you profoundly
Caught up in tongue twisters
Elegantly stu stu stuttering
While trying to sentence words

Imprisoning paragraphs
Causing phrases to breakout
Escaping in all forms
Leaving letters to fend for themselves
Spreading thin
Connecting to everything they touch
So Dare I say, outbreak
Because some letters connected to
U A, E, O and I didn't forget
About the physical stimulation
But this is intellectual love making...
It's like an addiction
And causes more friction
Flares flying high
Smoke vastly escapes
I'm Consumed
So Engulfed
By the fire we make

The Love I Have

When the sun sets and
The moon rises
I gaze into your eyes
No disguises
No surprises
First place prize
Love second to none
Finally winning
Life's just beginning
No longer spinning in this bubble
That held my life
Your love popped it
And I fell into your hands
And interrupted plans
Became one goal
Life took a stroll
And found the answer to
Love's equation
By adding us together
Then she put those little bars at our sides
You know,
To give us absolute value
But nothing can contain
The love I have for you

Spoken

Words are like water
Formless and abundant
Shapeless until
Spoken
Like bottling the ocean
This world flows
With utterances
Of words
Spoken

Reflection Section

Made in the USA
Columbia, SC
07 February 2019